STUDY GUIDE

9 STUDIES FOR
INDIVIDUALS AND GROUPS

MICHAEL CARD

WITH DALE AND SANDY LARSEN

InterVarsity Press
Downers Grove, Illinois

InterVarsity Press
P.O. Box 1400, Downers Grove, IL 60515-1426
World Wide Web: www.ivpress.com
E-mail: mail@ivpress.com

InterVarsity Press® is the book-publishing division of InterVarsity Christian Fellowship/USA®, a student
movement active on campus at hundreds of universities, colleges and schools of nursing in the United States of
America, and a member movement of the International Fellowship of Evangelical Students. For information
about local and regional activities, write Public Relations Dept., InterVarsity Christian Fellowship/USA, 6400
Schroeder Rd., P.O. Box 7895, Madison, WI 53707-7895, or visit the IVCF website at <www.ivcf.org>.

Unless otherwise indicated, all Scripture quotations are taken from the Holy Bible, New Living Translation,
copyright ©1996. Used by permission of Tyndale House Publishers, Inc., Wheaton, Illinois 60189. All rights
reserved.

Cover design: Cindy Kiple

Cover image: stone: Jim Linna/Getty Images
            ground/cracks for cross: Albert J. Copley/Getty Images
            hands: White Packert/Getty Images

ISBN 0-8308-2069-8

Printed in the United States of America ∞

P	17	16	15	14	13	12	11	10	9	8	7	6	5	4	3	2	1
Y	15	14	13	12	11	10	09	08	07	06	05	04	03				

Contents

INTRODUCTION

The Search for Simon

I was raised with a particular image of the apostle Simon Peter. For me he was the thoroughly humanized fisherman, possessing all the foibles and fragileness of any modern man. This was the Simon Peter of the seventies—a costar in *Jesus Christ Superstar*. He was portrayed as the one who consistently had his foot in his mouth, "old impetuous Peter." He's just like you and me, only more so.

During this same period of time, I received an opposite image of him. "Peter," the preachers would intone, "the Rock, strong and solid." In this version, Jesus chose Peter because of his robust character. Simon was just the type of person for whom he was looking.

But these images seemed conflicting, one-dimensional and incomplete to me. So which one was he?

Later, when Simon stepped fully formed from the pages of Acts, it was as if I had never before seen him in all my years of Bible study. He was more complex than I had ever imagined. I began to understand for the first time the wonderful progression in his character as a leader after the years of walking with Jesus. And their relationship! I had never understood just how close the two of them were, Jesus and Simon.

The Rock indeed he was. Jesus' words had proclaimed it so, and over the years of ministry he had grown by grace into the title. But he was a fragile stone still, completely dependent on his Master and Friend, even as Jesus had insisted on his own dependence on the Father. Certainly there was something solid in him, but it was Jesus' doing. And yes, he was like you and me—and again he was not. He stumbled, to be sure, lost his temper and said "no" to Jesus just as you and I do. But at the same time he was completely unique by virtue of the call that had been placed on his life. Sure, we all fall, but never to the degree Simon fell. And which of us will ever walk on the water?

For certain he was passionate, but not in the shallow, half-cocked way in which he had been portrayed to me. His was a passion that caused him to say more than he knew with a wisdom that even Jesus confessed was from heaven, or else with a foolishness so deep it could have only come from the pit. His was a passion that could murderously lash out, single-handed, against two hundred armed men. Or it could smolder, still white-hot, for the decades during which he left home and family again and again to speak Jesus' word and do his work.

In the Gospels Simon is properly the costar in the cast. He is the only other fully formed character in the Gospels besides Jesus. In Acts, at least in the first twelve chapters, he becomes the leading man. The lovable, perpetually misunderstanding and often misunderstood disciple of the Gospels has been transformed by the Spirit into the true foundational leader of the church.

But somewhere along the way we lost him. Or perhaps it might be better to say that at several points along the way (for whatever reason) his image became blurred beyond recognition. Now we need to go back to the Scriptures to refocus and recover a truer picture.

From the New Testament and from extrabiblical sources we know certain basic facts of Simon's life. But there is infinitely more to knowing a person than facts. We all possess an emotional and spiritual life as well, and nothing could be more evident in the biblical portrayal of Peter. Our emotional lives are expressed in the give and take of relationship as we come to know the true heart of another person, as true friendships are hammered out.

It is Peter's friendship with Jesus that we see most clearly and in the most detail in the Gospels. We read of their very first meeting, after which it seems that Peter seldom left Jesus' side. The tension that sometimes flares between the two—a tension which indeed exists in any genuine and deep relationship—is seen again and again. Peter is the only one of his disciples we hear rebuking Jesus, the only person who ever says "no" to him. Sometimes I wonder if Jesus didn't love him all the more for his passion. They were sometimes frustrated with each other, and yet they remained intimate friends.

When Jesus goes to struggle in Gethsemane, he takes the Three with him, but when he must come back three times to check on them, he speaks only to Peter. After the resurrection Jesus sends word, "Tell the disciples . . . and Peter." And shortly afterward Jesus first appears to Peter alone in a mysterious and unrecorded meeting.

Peter is fully himself, whatever Gospel you take up. His rich and complex character stays the same whatever Gospel you choose. He is the most human. Perhaps that's one reason Jesus seemed to be so attracted to him; indeed, it is the same reason we are still attracted to him today. It's a miracle, when you think about it, that Jesus would be able to choose a person whom so many of us could relate to, feel a kinship with and love.

Though it concerns me, I am not interested in examining what the reasons might be for Simon's disappearance from our contemporary Christian culture, but I do know I want to understand him better. I am fully aware of the tenuousness of writing about the emotional life of someone I am separated from by two thousand years. I am willing to confess that I don't really understand my own emotional life most of the time. So why, you are justified in asking, should I embark on this journey of seeking to understand Simon Peter's emotional life?

The answer is because of the portrayal of Peter in all of the Gospels. His emotional state is so often alluded to, if not spelled out, in the text. Because this information has been provided, I believe the writers mean for us to use it in understanding who Peter is.

My prayer is that together we will make this journey toward a better understanding of one of the most important figures of the New Testament— but not for the sake of understanding him alone. This would have been onerous to someone like Peter. No, the ultimate reason for getting to know Peter is so together we might better know Jesus. For the story of Peter is the story of Jesus. Perhaps, if you and I do our best, the same will be said of us someday.

ONE

A Meeting on the Seashore

A Fragile Stone Chapters 1 & 2
LUKE 5:1-11

So much of both their lives would be spent within the sight of that lake. Simon had spent most of his life on it, and the lake had given a measure of life to him. At least once it had almost taken both their lives. They would meet, and three years later, they would part ways beside this same lake, known as the "Sea of Galilee"—that body of water was the heart of the green and beautiful Galilee. This was the nexus of Simon's world.

It was a good location for a small fishing business. This was the world of Simon bar-Jonah and his brother Andrew. And so it was not in the high and holy place of Jerusalem but in green and obscure Galilee that Jesus and Simon's life together began.

We might imagine what he smelled like that morning, having fished all night, as was his custom. The pungent smell of the lake mixed with his sweat and the strong smell of fish—earthy, organic, common, repelling and somehow attracting all the same, like Simon himself. He would no doubt have had a fisherman's rough hands as well, though handshaking would not become customary for another thousand years.

The understanding gaze of Jesus was not focused on the externals of the curious fisherman that morning. He looked into and saw the heart of who Simon was and what he would become.

"You *are* Simon, the son of John," Jesus said. "But you *will be* called Cephas" (John 1:42).

Though Jesus bestows the new title of "Rock" (*Cephas* in Aramaic), he will never call Simon by that name because it is, after all, not a proper name. He is always Simon to Jesus. Only later, in Acts, will the name Simon give way to Peter, in the same way "Christ" is a title that later became a part of Jesus' name. Jesus Christ. Simon Peter. So Peter *(Cephas)* is not merely an affectionate nickname but a prophetic title that describes who Simon will, by grace, become, a new name signifying a new life.

But all of that lies ahead of this simple, confused fisherman. For now, he is still standing beside his familiar lake. He is holding not keys but smelly, soggy nets in chapped hands. Before him stands simply a new friend who seems to see him with understanding and sympathetic eyes. It is one of those ordinary, earth-shaking, timeless moments when two lives intersect. Simon Peter has no idea what lies ahead.

OPEN

When have you been thrust into a new identity, either in how others perceive you or how you perceive yourself?

How do you now see God's hand at work in the change? To what extent did you see it at the time?

STUDY

Jesus will never command the disciples to do something he has not first perfectly demonstrated in his own life. So if he intends to call on them to catch men, he will first show them how it is done. On this day it is Jesus who is fishing for men. He will cast his net and catch at least four, James and John, Andrew and, of course, Simon Peter. *Read Luke 5:1-11.*

¹One day as Jesus was preaching on the shore of the Sea of Galilee, great crowds pressed in on him to listen to the word of God. ²He noticed two empty boats at the water's edge, for the fishermen had left them and were washing their nets. ³Stepping into one of the boats, Jesus asked Simon, its owner, to push it out into the water. So he sat in the boat and taught the crowds from there.

⁴When he had finished speaking, he said to Simon, "Now go out where it is deeper and let down your nets, and you will catch many fish."

⁵"Master," Simon replied, "we worked hard all last night and didn't catch a thing. But if you say so, we'll try again." ⁶And this time their nets were so full they began to tear! ⁷A shout for help brought their partners in the other boat, and soon both boats were filled with fish and on the verge of sinking.

⁸When Simon Peter realized what had happened, he fell to his knees before Jesus and said, "Oh, Lord, please leave me—I'm too much of a sinner to be around you." ⁹For he was awe-struck by the size of their catch, as were the others with him. ¹⁰His partners, James and John, the sons of Zebedee, were also amazed.

Jesus replied to Simon, "Don't be afraid! From now on you'll be fishing for people!" ¹¹And as soon as they landed, they left everything and followed Jesus.

1. Throughout this passage, what attitude does Simon demonstrate toward Jesus?

2. How did Jesus make creative use of Simon's fishing boat (vv. 1-3)?

3. Why would Simon have been surprised at Jesus' command to go out and let down the nets again (v. 4)?

4. Why do you think Simon complied with Jesus' instructions (v. 5)?

5. The catch was unimaginable—enough to nearly sink two boats (vv. 6-7). Simon was "awestruck," but what he expressed to Jesus was stronger than awe. How do you explain his violently emotional reaction (vv. 8-9)?

What did he learn about Jesus?

Simon fears because he is a man who, thanks to the preaching of John, has become aware of his sinful state. And now he has become the beneficiary of Jesus, who has graciously filled his nets in spite of himself. There was nothing in his experience, nor in ours, that could have prepared him for this kind of frightening generosity. We are forever asking for the things we think we deserve. Simon knew then what we need to learn now: what we *deserve* is only death and separation from God and all his goodness. If we, for one blink, could step back and glimpse the awesome generosity of the One who should, by all rights, destroy us, we would join Simon on our knees with the same confession on our trembling lips.

6. Think of a time when you encountered Jesus in a startling, new way. When have you thought it might be preferable to have Jesus *not* get involved in a situation—that is, it would be more comfortable for things to stay as they are?

7. How did Jesus reassure Simon (v. 10)?

8. How has Jesus reassured you in times of radical change?

9. Simon, James and John "left everything" to follow Jesus (v. 11). What would have been some immediate costs of leaving everything?

10. Why do you think they were so willing to follow in such an extreme way?

11. In your own experience, what has made following Jesus worth the cost?

COMMIT

If we are to be honest, we'll admit that to follow—to really leave everything behind—is an absolutely terrifying prospect. Our most natural response would be, like Peter, to fall down and say, "Go away! This is more than I can deal with. I couldn't be the person you're looking for."

We stand before these terrifying possibilities—to let go of our security, to open ourselves to the frightening possibility of complete and utter success, to leave all that is familiar and safe for an unknown world. But then we notice that standing beside us is Jesus. He confidently whispers, "Don't be afraid. Let go of the nets. Do not be afraid. After all, it's me." Jesus has shown Simon that the sea he thought was empty was in fact full of fish. And Simon has begun to learn what it means to become partners with Jesus. A new kind of fishing is ahead.

Picture yourself standing on the shore of the lake with Jesus. What might Jesus be calling you to do? What might he ask you to leave behind? Pray for a deeper realization of his love, which will give you courage to let go of false security and follow in spite of the cost.

Thank the Lord for getting—and staying—involved in the details of your life. Pray that he will overcome any hesitation or fear of following him. Thank him for sudden changes that, over time, have proved to be blessings.

FOR FURTHER READING: chapters 1 & 2 of A Fragile Stone.

TWO

The Fearless Water Walker

A Fragile Stone Chapter 4
MATTHEW 14:22-33

On two separate occasions we see the disciples caught out in the Sea of Galilee. The first incident is the occasion of a violent storm. Matthew and Mark both tell of a second incident. In this story the disciples are caught in a strong wind, not a full-blown storm. Mark tells us they were straining against the oars, for the wind was against them.

But the difference between the two accounts is not the condition of the weather. The major difference is that in the first story Jesus is with them in the boat, though he is asleep. In this second account, the one before us now, he is nowhere to be seen.

Both Matthew and Mark tell us that Jesus, after he dismissed the crowd, had gone into the hills to pray. Only Mark's account (informed by Peter) gives us the detail that Jesus could see the disciples in their difficult situation. Both writers tell us Jesus left his prayers and walked on the water to be with his men. If they are caught in a struggle, he wants to be there with them.

It was almost dawn, the fourth or last watch of the night. Only Peter gives us the mystifying detail that Jesus was about to pass by them. When they all saw him, walking on the water, they drew what, if you think about it, was a fairly logical conclusion. They thought they were seeing a ghost. What else would walk on the water in the middle of such a scary, windy night?

Peter remembers the former angry storm and Jesus' rebuke, "How is it that you have no faith?" He is determined now that he will not hear those words again from Jesus (Mark 4:35-41). "If it is you," he says, "tell me to come to you on the water."

Open

What are some seemingly impossible obstacles you have faced?

What range of emotions did you go through as you faced the obstacle?

Study

Read Matthew 14:22-33. ("Immediately after this" refers to the miraculous feeding of 5,000+ people with five loaves of bread and two fish.)

22Immediately after this, Jesus made his disciples get back into the boat and cross to the other side of the lake while he sent the people home. 23Afterward he went up into the hills by himself to pray. Night fell while he was there alone. 24Meanwhile, the disciples were in trouble far away from land, for a strong wind had risen, and they were fighting heavy waves.

25About three o'clock in the morning Jesus came to them, walking on the water. 26When the disciples saw him, they screamed in terror, thinking he was a ghost. 27But Jesus spoke to them at once. "It's all right," he said. "I am here! Don't be afraid."

28Then Peter called to him, "Lord, if it's really you, tell me to come to you by walking on water."

29"All right, come," Jesus said.

So Peter went over the side of the boat and walked on the water toward Jesus. 30But when he looked around at the high waves, he was terrified and began to sink. "Save me, Lord!" he shouted.

31Instantly Jesus reached out his hand and grabbed him. "You don't have much faith," Jesus said. "Why did you doubt me?" 32And when they climbed back into the boat, the wind stopped.

33Then the disciples worshiped him. "You really are the Son of God!" they exclaimed.

1. Point out some characteristics of Simon Peter that reveal themselves in this passage.

2. Imagine that you are Simon, out in that boat at night with the wind kicking up high waves. Jesus sent you out here while he remained onshore. What is going through your mind?

3. Already edgy because of the wind, the disciples "screamed in terror" when they thought they saw a ghost (v. 26). How do you think they responded to Jesus' words in verse 27?

4. How do you explain Peter's words and actions in verses 28-29?

What sort of person wants to walk on the water in the middle of a dark windstorm? Was he motivated by some innate desire to do what he saw Jesus doing? Or did he want to walk on the water simply so he could be with

Jesus? Whatever the reason, Peter often wants to do the wrong thing for the
right reason. All of us sometimes ask to do things that we do not have the
faith to do. Was Peter's request courage or insanity or a little bit of both?
The courage and foolishness of faith? What often goes unappreciated is the
fact that Peter's short walk was indeed a triumph of faith. It is his first miracle! Was this not an astounding experiment?

5. What went suddenly wrong, and why (v. 30)?

6. How did Jesus show his mercy to Peter (vv. 31-32)?

7. When has the Lord reached out and caught you when your faith faltered?

8. How did these remarkable events change the disciples' perception of
   who Jesus was (v. 33)?

9. What kinds of landmark events have changed your perception of Jesus?

COMMIT

Worship is the language of our new reality. But we must never forget that it always begins with a cry for help. It ends when we find ourselves doing the unreal and impossible, when we discover that we, if even for a moment, have risen above the noise of the wind and the confusion of the waves. We find in the darkness a Face. We discover in the tumult a Hand. And we worship him for it all.

Consider times that you have "done the impossible" with the Lord's help. Consider also times that your faith has faltered and the Lord has shown you his mercy. Let the memory of those times lead you into worship of him. Commit difficult areas of your life to him, in trust that "I can do everything through him who gives me strength" (Philippians 4:13 NIV).

Pray for the courage to take action on the faith you have, whether great or small.

FOR FURTHER READING: chapter 4 of *A Fragile Stone.*

THREE

Who They Both Are

A Fragile Stone Chapters 5 & 6
MATTHEW 16:13-23

If Jesus can be said to have had a best friend, it was certainly Simon Peter. It has been my experience that friends define each other. When I am uncertain about the direction of my life, I go to my closest friends to affirm, or perhaps reaffirm, who I am and what the calling on my life is all about.

What we see between Simon and Jesus is not unlike that. Certainly Jesus does not need to be told who he is. But perhaps in his humanity there was still from time to time the hunger for the assurance of his friend. And beyond a doubt Peter needed the defining presence of Jesus in his life, as we all do. As Peter's circle of friends expands with his ministry, we will see him doing the same thing in his letters. Again and again, he writes telling us who we are: strangers, a royal priesthood, God's elect. That is what friends do. They help each other understand who they are. Jesus and Peter are both rocks in their own unique ways—Jesus, forever the solid Rock (Psalm 18:31; Isaiah 26:4; 44:8); Simon, always (but by grace) the fragile stone. In the intimacy of their sometimes volatile friendship they will strive to reflect the truth of who they are to each other for the short amount of time they have left.

OPEN

How do you usually think of Jesus? What comes to mind? When have you come to realize in a fresher or deeper way that Jesus is

• Savior?

• Lord?

• Friend?

• the Good Shepherd?

• God incarnate?

• some other title or identity? _____

What differences has your new insight made in your relationships? in your worship?

STUDY

Read Matthew 16:13-23.

¹³*When Jesus came to the region of Caesarea Philippi, he asked his disciples, "Who do people say that the Son of Man is?"*

¹⁴*"Well," they replied, "some say John the Baptist, some say Elijah, and others say Jeremiah or one of the other prophets."*

¹⁵*Then he asked them, "Who do you say I am?"*

¹⁶*Simon Peter answered, "You are the Messiah, the Son of the living God."*

¹⁷*Jesus replied, "You are blessed, Simon son of John, because my Father in heaven has revealed this to you. You did not learn this from any human being. ¹⁸Now I say to you that you are Peter, and upon this rock I will build my church, and all the powers of hell will not conquer it. ¹⁹And I will give you the keys of the Kingdom of Heaven. Whatever you lock on earth will be locked in heaven, and whatever you open on earth will be opened in heaven." ²⁰Then he sternly warned them not to tell anyone that he was the Messiah.*

²¹*From then on Jesus began to tell his disciples plainly that he had to go to Jerusalem, and*

he told them what would happen to him there. He would suffer at the hands of the leaders and the leading priests and the teachers of religious law. He would be killed, and he would be raised on the third day.

²²But Peter took him aside and corrected him. "Heaven forbid, Lord," he said. "This will never happen to you!"

²³Jesus turned to Peter and said, "Get away from me, Satan! You are a dangerous trap to me. You are seeing things merely from a human point of view, and not from God's."

1. Sketch or chart the succession of moods you sense in Peter during this conversation with Jesus.

2. What contrast do you see between the two questions Jesus put to the disciples (vv. 13-15)?

3. How did Jesus affirm the rightness of Peter's answer (vv. 16-20)?

4. Once Peter had identified Jesus, how did Jesus bestow a new identity on Peter (vv. 18-19)?

"You are Peter," Jesus echoes back. It is the title, the promise he spoke when he first laid eyes on Simon. It is the name he affirmed when he called him to be a disciple. Now, in light of Simon's confession, he will explain what the title will come to mean. "On this rock I will build my church."

5. Jesus confirmed that he was the Messiah, the Jewish people's long-awaited Anointed One, their Savior. When he went on to describe his future (v. 21), what impact would his words have had on these Jewish disciples?

6. In verse 22 Peter seems to be calling Jesus a liar. Why would he dare to contradict Jesus the Messiah's own words about himself?

7. Jesus had just told Peter that he would be the foundation of the church. How could he address Peter as "Satan" in verse 23?

8. In what senses was Peter looking at Jesus "merely from a human point of view, and not from God's" (v. 23)?

9. Why is the idea of a comfortable, suffering-free Messiah a "dangerous trap" for Jesus (v. 23)?

10. In your own life, when does it seem easier to see Jesus from only a human point of view?

11. What brings you back to the reality of Jesus the suffering Messiah?

COMMIT

You would no doubt confess that Jesus is your friend. If that is true, then my question is, "How does he define you?" He began defining us all when he told us we were sinners. Then he gave us a hunger to know him, and we followed. But how long ago was that? And in the meantime, what has the complexion of your friendship looked like?

In Revelation 2:17 he hints at the fact that someday he will give us a white stone with a new name, our new name. Perhaps for Simon his was Peter, and Jesus simply could not wait to let him know. But what do you think your name might be? What will he call you? What will he call me?

In what areas of life are you willing to be identified with a suffering Christ? In what areas of life do you prefer to have a Christ who is easy and comfortable? How might Jesus be defining you? How might you declare his identity to others?

Pray that you will always be a help and not a hindrance to Jesus. Ask him to help you become who he has called you to be.

FOR FURTHER READING: chapters 5 & 6 of *A Fragile Stone*.

FOUR

"Fear Not!"

A Fragile Stone Chapter 7
MARK 9:2-10

Like so many other stories in the Gospels, the account usually referred to as "Jesus and the disciples on the mount of transfiguration" is really the story of Jesus and Peter on the mount. Though James and John are certainly there, we never hear a single word from them.

The experience was absolutely a defining moment for Simon. Jesus is transfigured. But Peter is transformed! The sight of Jesus in his true glory confirms that Peter's earlier confession was true. Jesus is the Messiah! He is the glorious Son of the living God.

The account comes and goes in a flash, like the burst of light that was Jesus' transfigured face. This is not a transformation—that is, Jesus does not change his form. Rather, the Three are allowed to see Jesus' true nature, as he has been all along, only their eyes have just now been opened. The veil is lifted for a few precious minutes.

OPEN

How would you feel about having your true nature revealed to others?

__ That's a frightening prospect.

__ It would depend on who the "others" were.

__ I have mixed feelings.

__ I wish it could happen.

__ I don't know if it's possible.

__ Other response:

Have you ever wished you could see the nature of Christ more clearly? What do you think the results would be?

STUDY

Read Mark 9:2-10. ("Six days later" means after Peter's confession that Jesus is the Christ.)

> *²Six days later Jesus took Peter, James, and John to the top of a mountain. No one else was there. As the men watched, Jesus' appearance changed, ³and his clothing became dazzling white, far whiter than any earthly process could ever make it. ⁴Then Elijah and Moses appeared and began talking with Jesus.*
>
> *⁵"Teacher, this is wonderful!" Peter exclaimed. "We will make three shrines—one for you, one for Moses, and one for Elijah." ⁶He didn't really know what to say, for they were all terribly afraid.*
>
> *⁷Then a cloud came over them, and a voice from the cloud said, "This is my beloved Son. Listen to him." ⁸Suddenly they looked around, and Moses and Elijah were gone, and only Jesus was with them. ⁹As they descended the mountainside, he told them not to tell anyone what they had seen until he, the Son of Man, had risen from the dead. ¹⁰So they kept it to themselves, but they often asked each other what he meant by "rising from the dead."*

1. Jesus had allowed only Peter, James and John to accompany him at a healing (Mark 5:37). Peter had identified Jesus as the Messiah. What do you think Peter expected when Jesus asked him and the others to go up the mountain with him (v. 2)?

2. Imagine that you are Peter on that mountaintop. One minute Jesus

looks normal; the next minute he is clothed in dazzling light. Then Moses and Elijah appear with him! What terrifies you most about all this (v. 6) and why?

3. What would Jesus' radiant appearance signify to Peter and the others (vv. 2-3)?

What the Three are witnessing is nothing less than unveiled glory. Peter has made his confession, has faced his moment of loyal despair, and now he experiences a vision of who Jesus really is. It is not as though Jesus was transformed, but more that a veil was momentarily removed. This is who Jesus has been all along. Now Peter sees it—and he is never the same again.

4. Have you ever experienced what I call "the terrifying splendor of Jesus" (perhaps not in a physical vision but in some other way)? How has the experience changed you and the way you think of Christ?

5. Why do you think Peter came up with the unusual suggestion in verse 5?

6. How did God the Father mercifully interrupt Peter's remarks (v. 7)?

7. You may have heard an unbeliever say, "If God would just show himself to me, I'd believe." How does this Scripture answer such a challenge?

8. Describe the emotions that must have swept over the disciples when they dared to look again (v. 8).

9. Jesus' glory has just been revealed to the disciples. The Gospel writer Matthew tells us that after Moses and Elijah were gone, Jesus touched the disciples and told them, "Don't be afraid" (Matthew 17:7). What else do Jesus' words reveal about him?

10. What does it mean to you to know that you do not have to be afraid of God?

On that mount Peter and the others got a glimpse into heaven. He discovered that not all mysteries will be explained there, but instead we will know how truly vast and unknowable the mystery of Christ is. Of all that he might have recounted, this incident on the mount is the only historical experience with Jesus to which Peter refers in his letters (2 Peter 1:16-18).

COMMIT

Where do you especially need to hear the Lord say, "Don't be afraid"?

Brennan Manning says, "If you don't have to be afraid of God, you don't have to be afraid of anything." How do you respond to that assertion? Make notes about your response.

Turn your notes into a prayer of trust and thankfulness to God for his generous grace in Christ.

Pray for people who are afraid to approach God. Ask him to give them assurance that they will find a warm welcome in his love.

FOR FURTHER READING: chapter 7 of *A Fragile Stone.*

FIVE

Confusion at the Final Meal

A Fragile Stone Chapter 9
JOHN 13:1-11

It was the beginning of an extraordinary day. Jesus sent Peter and John to make the extensive preparations for the Passover meal (Luke 22:7). They were sent to purchase bitter herbs, parsley, wine and *charoset*, a mixture of ground apples, raisins, almonds and cinnamon that symbolized the mortar their ancestors were forced to mix in Egypt. Most important, they would have chosen a lamb and had it certified as "spotless" by a priest at the temple. Did either of them see any connection between the innocent creature they purchased that morning and the one who awaited them when they returned from their errands?

OPEN

Where do you find it easiest to be a servant for other people? Where do you find it most difficult? How do you account for the difference?

STUDY

Read John 13:1-11.

¹*Before the Passover celebration, Jesus knew that his hour had come to leave this world and return to his Father. He now showed the disciples the full extent of his love.* ²*It was time for*

supper, and the Devil had already enticed Judas, son of Simon Iscariot, to carry out his plan to betray Jesus. ³Jesus knew that the Father had given him authority over everything and that he had come from God and would return to God. ⁴So he got up from the table, took off his robe, wrapped a towel around his waist, ⁵and poured water into a basin. Then he began to wash the disciples' feet and to wipe them with the towel he had around him.

⁶When he came to Simon Peter, Peter said to him, "Lord, why are you going to wash my feet?"

⁷Jesus replied, "You don't understand now why I am doing it; someday you will."

⁸"No," Peter protested, "you will never wash my feet!"

Jesus replied, "But if I don't wash you, you won't belong to me."

⁹Simon Peter exclaimed, "Then wash my hands and head as well, Lord, not just my feet!"

¹⁰Jesus replied, "A person who has bathed all over does not need to wash, except for the feet, to be entirely clean. And you are clean, but that isn't true of everyone here." ¹¹For Jesus knew who would betray him. That is what he meant when he said, "Not all of you are clean."

1. What surprising actions did Jesus take at the Passover meal?

2. According to this Scripture, why did Jesus do what he did?

3. How did Peter react when Jesus approached him with the basin and towel (v. 6)?

4. For the past several years, Peter had watched Jesus selflessly serve others, including the outcasts of society. Why would he now object to seeing Jesus in this servant role?

5. Jesus assured Peter that someday he would understand (v. 7). How did his words affect Peter (v. 8)?

Peter was right! It was inappropriate for Jesus to be doing what he was doing. In Simon's and everyone else's mind the Messiah would never suffer, never submit, never serve. By the end of this long day Jesus will have done all three.

6. In verses 8-9 Peter goes from absolute no to absolute yes. What changed his mind about having Jesus wash his feet?

7. How did Jesus reveal his knowledge of all the disciples' hearts (vv. 10-11)?

8. When have you realized that you needed to be "washed" (forgiven of your sin) by Christ?

9. How does the knowledge of our own sinfulness make us more willing servants?

10. (private question) Where do you most identify with Peter's words in verse 9?

COMMIT

Luke tells us that after a dispute about who was the greatest (and presumably after John's account of the footwashing), Jesus sums up the lesson in humility. "But among you, those who are the greatest should take the lowest rank, and the leader should be like a servant. Normally the master sits at the table and is served by his servants. But not here! For I am your servant" (Luke 22:26-27).

Privately identify people whom you would rather *not* serve in humility. Prayerfully search your heart and ask yourself, "Am I self-righteous? Do I feel I am better than those people? Where is my attitude not Christlike? How might I serve them?"

Pray for a servant heart even toward those you would prefer not to serve. Thank the Lord for washing you from your sins, even the sin of self-righteousness. Praise him for his undeserved mercy.

FOR FURTHER READING: chapter 9 of *A Fragile Stone*.

SIX

The Despairing Denier

A *Fragile Stone* Chapters 10 & 11
MARK 14:27-42, 66-72

All four Gospels tell the story of Peter's denial. It was an important message for the early church, faced as they were with the same temptation to deny Jesus before their Roman persecutors. It is also the vital key to understanding the rest of Peter's life. The heartbreaking denials provide an emotional window into the heart of the man he would become. It broke Peter in the best sense of the word.

Each Evangelist accounts for the three denials—two initial queries followed an hour later by a third, more direct confrontation that causes Peter not to curse but to swear an oath, something Jesus had urged them never to do (Matthew 5:37). But we will begin hours before that, immediately after the Last Supper.

OPEN

When and where are you least comfortable being identified as a follower of Christ?

___ at work

___ at school

___ in community involvements, such as _____

___ with certain family members

___ in a public leadership role

___ in a situation where people are making fun of Christians

___ other circumstances:

What do you think would help you be more open about your faith?

STUDY

Jesus and the disciples (all except Judas) were on their way to the garden called Gethsemane. Jesus once again made a prediction that his disciples would fail to stand by him. *Read Mark 14:27-42.*

> ²⁷*"All of you will desert me," Jesus told them. "For the Scriptures say,*
> *'God will strike the Shepherd,*
> *and the sheep will be scattered.'*
> ²⁸*But after I am raised from the dead, I will go ahead of you to Galilee and meet you there."*
> ²⁹*Peter said to him, "Even if everyone else deserts you, I never will."*
> ³⁰*"Peter," Jesus replied, "the truth is, this very night, before the rooster crows twice, you will deny me three times."*
> ³¹*"No!" Peter insisted. "Not even if I have to die with you! I will never deny you!" And all the others vowed the same.*
> ³²*And they came to an olive grove called Gethsemane, and Jesus said, "Sit here while I go and pray."* ³³*He took Peter, James, and John with him, and he began to be filled with horror and deep distress.* ³⁴*He told them, "My soul is crushed with grief to the point of death. Stay here and watch with me."*
> ³⁵*He went on a little farther and fell face down on the ground. He prayed that, if it were possible, the awful hour awaiting him might pass him by.* ³⁶*"Abba, Father," he said, "everything is possible for you. Please take this cup of suffering away from me. Yet I want your will, not mine."*
> ³⁷*Then he returned and found the disciples asleep. "Simon!" he said to Peter. "Are you asleep? Couldn't you stay awake and watch with me even one hour?* ³⁸*Keep alert and pray. Otherwise temptation will overpower you. For though the spirit is willing enough, the body is weak."*
> ³⁹*Then Jesus left them again and prayed, repeating his pleadings.* ⁴⁰*Again he returned to them and found them sleeping, for they just couldn't keep their eyes open. And they didn't know what to say.*

⁴¹When he returned to them the third time, he said, "Still sleeping? Still resting? Enough! The time has come. I, the Son of Man, am betrayed into the hands of sinners. ⁴²Up, let's be going. See, my betrayer is here!"

1. Trace Peter's part in this account. Where is he, what is he doing, and what does he say?

2. With what attitude does Peter meet Jesus' statement that they will all desert him (vv. 7-31)?

3. Have you ever been completely sure that you would never deny Christ— but then you failed? How do you account for your failure?

4. Jesus had taken Peter, James and John with him to a healing and to see him transfigured. Now a sense of foreboding hangs over the disciples and Jesus. What do you think Peter expected when Jesus took the three of them into the garden to pray (vv. 32- 33)?

5. Imagine that you are Peter, instructed by Jesus to stay awake and watch, and he returns to catch you sleeping *three* times (vv. 37, 40-41)! What do

you think, and how do you feel each time he wakes you?

When Judas and the crowd of soldiers and officials arrived, Jesus met them bravely and calmly. Peter lunged forward with a sword and slashed off a piece of one man's ear, which Jesus healed. In disbelief Peter saw Jesus bound and led away. As the Lord had predicted, the disciples deserted him and fled. But Peter remembered his vow to follow him to the death. He and John shadowed the mob to the house of the high priest, Caiaphas, where Jesus was being interrogated and accused. *Read Mark 14:66-72.*

⁶⁶Meanwhile, Peter was below in the courtyard. One of the servant girls who worked for the high priest ⁶⁷noticed Peter warming himself at the fire. She looked at him closely and then said, "You were one of those with Jesus, the Nazarene."

⁶⁸Peter denied it. "I don't know what you're talking about," he said, and he went out into the entryway. Just then, a rooster crowed.

⁶⁹The servant girl saw him standing there and began telling the others, "That man is definitely one of them!" ⁷⁰Peter denied it again.

A little later some other bystanders began saying to Peter, "You must be one of them because you are from Galilee."

⁷¹Peter said, "I swear by God, I don't know this man you're talking about." ⁷²And immediately the rooster crowed the second time. Suddenly, Jesus' words flashed through Peter's mind: "Before the rooster crows twice, you will deny me three times." And he broke down and cried.

Peter and John were right inside the high priest's courtyard. John tells us that the Jewish officials themselves had kindled the fire, and Peter was standing among them warming himself (John 18:18)! What does Peter's behavior say to you about his loyalty to Jesus?

6. Considering the risk Peter took to stand there in the high priest's courtyard, how do you account for his first denial (vv. 66-68)?

7. Peter heard the rooster crow the first time as Jesus had predicted (v. 68),
but he went on to deny the Lord twice more. We can sense his growing
panic (vv. 69-71) as he is pressed by questions until he insists, "I don't
know this man you're talking about." Why do you think he did not recall
Jesus' words until he heard the rooster crow the second time (v. 72)?

8. Go back to your answer to question 3. How has Christ restored you after
your failure(s)?

COMMIT

There is a wonderful quality about having our corporate identity in someone like Simon. He is us! Jesus could have chosen no one better. Even as he
cried out when he began to sink into the sea, so now as he begins to sink into
his own despair Peter goes out and weeps bitterly. He cries once more and
will once more be rescued and forgiven by Jesus.

Consider those situations where you are reluctant to confess that you
belong to Christ. Bring each of them to him in confession. Prayerfully consider why each one intimidates you. Ask the Lord for a special sense of his
presence and encouragement when you next go into any of those situations.

Pray that you will keep alert and stay on guard against the temptation to deny Christ.

FOR FURTHER READING: chapters 10 & 11 of *A Fragile Stone.*

SEVEN

New Hope on the Seashore

A *Fragile Stone* Chapter 13
JOHN 21:1-19

The disciples' nets were once again empty, as empty as their hearts and souls. It was almost as if their last three years together had never really happened. Here they were, back where they started on the calm morning lake with empty nets after working all night. What was it he had said? Fishers of *men*?

Jesus appeared to Peter again where it all began three years earlier, on the shore of the lake. Peter, who was to fish for men, was fishing, unsuccessfully, once more for fish. It was almost as if nothing had happened. But all at once there he stood, not in glory with the legions of angels he said he commanded but by a waning fire he himself had built with those ruined hands.

OPEN
Consider a time that God unexpectedly gave you back something you thought was lost. How did you respond?

__ I couldn't thank him enough.

__ I felt undeserving.

__ I wondered if it was really true.

__ I tried to find a reason.

__ I wondered if there was a catch to it.

__ Other response:

Study

Read John 21:1-19.

¹*Later Jesus appeared again to the disciples beside the Sea of Galilee. This is how it happened.* ²*Several of the disciples were there—Simon Peter, Thomas (nicknamed the Twin), Nathanael from Cana in Galilee, the sons of Zebedee, and two other disciples.*

³*Simon Peter said, "I'm going fishing."*

"We'll come, too," they all said. So they went out in the boat, but they caught nothing all night. ⁴*At dawn the disciples saw Jesus standing on the beach, but they couldn't see who he was.* ⁵*He called out, "Friends, have you caught any fish?"*

"No," they replied.

⁶*Then he said, "Throw out your net on the right-hand side of the boat, and you'll get plenty of fish!" So they did, and they couldn't draw in the net because there were so many fish in it.* ⁷*Then the disciple whom Jesus loved said to Peter, "It is the Lord!" When Simon Peter heard that it was the Lord, he put on his tunic (for he had stripped for work), jumped into the water, and swam ashore.* ⁸*The others stayed with the boat and pulled the loaded net to the shore, for they were only out about three hundred feet.* ⁹*When they got there, they saw that a charcoal fire was burning and fish were frying over it, and there was bread.*

¹⁰*"Bring some of the fish you've just caught," Jesus said.* ¹¹*So Simon Peter went aboard and dragged the net to the shore. There were 153 large fish, and yet the net hadn't torn.*

¹²*"Now come and have some breakfast!" Jesus said. And no one dared ask him if he really was the Lord because they were sure of it.* ¹³*Then Jesus served them the bread and the fish.* ¹⁴*This was the third time Jesus had appeared to his disciples since he had been raised from the dead.*

¹⁵*After breakfast Jesus said to Simon Peter, "Simon son of John, do you love me more than these?"*

"Yes, Lord," Peter replied, "you know I love you."

"Then feed my lambs," Jesus told him.

¹⁶*Jesus repeated the question: "Simon son of John, do you love me?"*

"Yes, Lord," Peter said, "you know I love you."

"Then take care of my sheep," Jesus said.

¹⁷*Once more he asked him, "Simon son of John, do you love me?"*

Peter was grieved that Jesus asked the question a third time. He said, "Lord, you know everything. You know I love you."

Jesus said, "Then feed my sheep. ¹⁸The truth is, when you were young, you were able to do as you liked and go wherever you wanted to. But when you are old, you will stretch out your hands, and others will direct you and take you where you don't want to go." ¹⁹Jesus said this to let him know what kind of death he would die to glorify God. Then Jesus told him, "Follow me."

1. How do the circumstances in this story compare with the circumstances in Luke 5:1-11 (study 1)?

2. Make a line graph or diagram of Peter's emotions (as nearly as you can discern them) during these events.

3. How do you think John recognized that "it is the Lord!" (v. 7)?

4. What words or phrases would you use to describe Peter's leap into the water and swim to shore?

5. When have you been overwhelmingly eager to "get to" Christ (not physically but spiritually)?

6. After breakfast, how did Jesus question Peter, and how did Peter respond (vv. 15-17)?

7. Peter had been a fisherman, not a shepherd. How might he have inter-
   preted Jesus' three commands in verses 15-17?

8. Who are the "sheep" and "lambs" God is calling you to feed and care for?

9. Jesus gave Peter a glimpse of how his life would end (vv. 18-19). What
   effect do you think his words had on Peter?

10. When you reach the end of your life, of what would you like to be cer-
    tain?

COMMIT

They had first met beside this very same sea, on this same shore. At first Jesus had to show Simon that the lake he thought was empty was indeed full of fish. Now a new kind of fisherman is left standing there—beside not a lake of fish but a vast sea of souls. He will fish for men and women. He will tend and feed the flock of Jesus. He can accomplish all this now because, in his brokenness, he knows the certainty both of his love for Jesus and—more importantly—of Jesus' love for him. He is armed with the painful knowing of his own end. He is ready.

Look again at your answer to question 2. On your chart, mark the places where you think you have ever felt the way Peter felt, even if the circumstances were very different. When have you been far from God, and how has Jesus restored his relationship with you?

Write out your thoughts about this question: If Jesus asked you "Do you love me?" how would you respond?

Pray prayers of thanks that regardless of the ups and downs of our experiences and feelings, Christ calls out to us and offers us forgiveness. Pray for the sheep and lambs God has called you to care for.

FOR FURTHER READING: chapter 13 of *A Fragile Stone.*

EIGHT

The Reluctant Reconciler

A *Fragile Stone* Chapter 17
ACTS 10:1-36

When I visited First Missionary Baptist Church, I was the only white person in the sanctuary. Though I had been meeting there for a year or more to pray with the men of the Empty Hands Fellowship (along with Dr. William Lane), this was a different situation altogether. As I walked in, an elderly woman came up to me and asked, "Why are you here?" It was not an angry question. She really wanted to know. And I could not give her a good answer. I could only stammer, "I'm a friend of Denny's."

I sat in the back, in the only empty seat I could find. I was nervous. Several people around me felt the same way. As the service began we sang some of the songs I remembered from another black church I had attended. That helped calm my nerves. As Denny began his sermon an elderly woman I was sitting next to took my hand in hers. At first I didn't know what to do, so I did nothing at all. Every time the preacher would make a point she would give my hand a squeeze. She was unaware of what she was doing. I learned later that she and her husband had raised over forty foster children. Dinah quite simply is a magnet who draws to herself people to love. Whenever she is asked why she adopted so many children she responds, "Who else is going to love them if not me?"

That Sunday morning I became one of her children. She and her husband, Bob, had numbered white children as well among their extended family. With the reach of her hand I was also accepted. Though it has been years, I still have not found my way completely into the congregation, though I am always more than welcomed. Some lines take years to cross. I can only tell you that my awkward attempt at racial reconciliation is a response to a fragmented part of my life, a piece of a puzzle that may never fully come together. All I know is something in me longs to find a place for it to fit.

There comes a moment in our lives when some of the pieces of the puzzle come together—where all our past experiences, both good and bad, are brought to bear in causing us to become who God intends us to be. The encounter of Cornelius was just such a moment in Peter's life.

OPEN

In what sort of church, and with what sort of Christians, are you most comfortable? Why?

In what sort of church, and with what sort of Christians, are you least comfortable? Why?

STUDY

Read Acts 10:1-36.

¹*In Caesarea there lived a Roman army officer named Cornelius, who was a captain of the Italian Regiment.* ²*He was a devout man who feared the God of Israel, as did his entire household. He gave generously to charity and was a man who regularly prayed to God.* ³*One afternoon about three o'clock, he had a vision in which he saw an angel of God coming toward him. "Cornelius!" the angel said.*

⁴*Cornelius stared at him in terror. "What is it, sir?" he asked the angel.*

And the angel replied, "Your prayers and gifts to the poor have not gone unnoticed by God!

⁵Now send some men down to Joppa to find a man named Simon Peter. ⁶He is staying with Simon, a leatherworker who lives near the shore. Ask him to come and visit you."

⁷As soon as the angel was gone, Cornelius called two of his household servants and a devout soldier, one of his personal attendants. ⁸He told them what had happened and sent them off to Joppa.

⁹The next day as Cornelius's messengers were nearing the city, Peter went up to the flat roof to pray. It was about noon, ¹⁰and he was hungry. But while lunch was being prepared, he fell into a trance. ¹¹He saw the sky open, and something like a large sheet was let down by its four corners. ¹²In the sheet were all sorts of animals, reptiles, and birds. ¹³Then a voice said to him, "Get up, Peter; kill and eat them."

¹⁴"Never, Lord," Peter declared. "I have never in all my life eaten anything forbidden by our Jewish laws."

¹⁵The voice spoke again, "If God says something is acceptable, don't say it isn't." ¹⁶The same vision was repeated three times. Then the sheet was pulled up again to heaven.

¹⁷Peter was very perplexed. What could the vision mean? Just then the men sent by Cornelius found the house and stood outside at the gate. ¹⁸They asked if this was the place where Simon Peter was staying. ¹⁹Meanwhile, as Peter was puzzling over the vision, the Holy Spirit said to him, "Three men have come looking for you. ²⁰Go down and go with them without hesitation. All is well, for I have sent them."

²¹So Peter went down and said, "I'm the man you are looking for. Why have you come?"

²²They said, "We were sent by Cornelius, a Roman officer. He is a devout man who fears the God of Israel and is well respected by all the Jews. A holy angel instructed him to send for you so you can go to his house and give him a message." ²³So Peter invited the men to be his guests for the night. The next day he went with them, accompanied by some other believers from Joppa.

²⁴They arrived in Caesarea the following day. Cornelius was waiting for him and had called together his relatives and close friends to meet Peter. ²⁵As Peter entered his home, Cornelius fell to the floor before him in worship. ²⁶But Peter pulled him up and said, "Stand up! I'm a human being like you!" ²⁷So Cornelius got up, and they talked together and went inside where the others were assembled.

²⁸Peter told them, "You know it is against the Jewish laws for me to come into a Gentile home like this. But God has shown me that I should never think of anyone as impure. ²⁹So I came as soon as I was sent for. Now tell me why you sent for me."

[30]Cornelius replied, "Four days ago I was praying in my house at three o'clock in the afternoon. Suddenly, a man in dazzling clothes was standing in front of me. [31]He told me, 'Cornelius, your prayers have been heard, and your gifts to the poor have been noticed by God! [32]Now send some men to Joppa and summon Simon Peter. He is staying in the home of Simon, a leatherworker who lives near the shore.' [33]So I sent for you at once, and it was good of you to come. Now here we are, waiting before God to hear the message the Lord has given you."

[34]Then Peter replied, "I see very clearly that God doesn't show partiality. [35]In every nation he accepts those who fear him and do what is right. [36]I'm sure you have heard about the Good News for the people of Israel—that there is peace with God through Jesus Christ, who is Lord of all."

1. Trace the events and the comings and goings in the different locations in this story.

2. What do we learn about Cornelius from vv. 1-2?

3. The angel could have told Cornelius about Christ directly (vv. 1-6). What advantages do you see in the roundabout way Cornelius heard the gospel?

4. How did the Holy Spirit begin to prepare Peter for the invitation to Cornelius's home (vv. 7-20)?

5. What was the message of the vision of the large sheet full of all sorts of animals (vv. 10-16)?

6. When and how has the Holy Spirit begun to open your mind and heart to Christians who do things differently from you?

For almost fifteen years Christianity had existed solely as a sect within Judaism, and for the most part its locus of faith was still the temple in Jerusalem. There were still those in leadership in the church who desired that things stay that way. With the Cornelius affair, matters will come to a point of crisis. The simple fact that the story is told twice, almost in its entirety, should tell us something significant is happening.

7. What is remarkable about the fact that Peter invited the men to stay overnight (vv. 21-23)?

8. Just as the angel could have told Cornelius the gospel directly, Peter could have told the three men the gospel and sent them back to Cornelius. How would both Peter and Cornelius benefit from Peter's making the journey to Caesarea (v. 23)?

9. How did Cornelius demonstrate his confidence in the Lord and in Peter (vv. 24-33)?

10. At what point do you think Peter finally got the message that Christ died for the Gentiles as well as for the Jews (vv. 28-36)?

11. When have you realized—perhaps in a flash of insight or perhaps gradually—that God loves and accepts a group of people you consider less than desirable? How has the realization changed you?

How has the realization changed your worship of God?

COMMIT

Peter didn't even make it through his sermon before the Holy Spirit, who so longs to embrace all men and women, interrupted him and poured himself out on them all. This was completely a work of God, Peter realized. It is a lesson he would carry with him all his life.

Go back to your answer to the second question under "Open." Try to identify how your Christian life would be different if you not only accepted but freely associated with those believers who now make you uncomfortable. What is most threatening about that prospect? What is most liberating about it?

If possible, make definite plans to join some of those Christians for worship or fellowship.

Pray for the wisdom to understand and the grace to accept believers who do not do things your way. Pray that you will become an agent of God's reconciliation.

FOR FURTHER READING: chapter 17 of *A Fragile Stone.*

NINE

The Passionate Writer

A *Fragile Stone* Chapter 18 & Epilogue
1 PETER 3:8-9; 2 PETER 1:5-8

Peter's letters are a remarkable mirror to the sermons of Peter in Acts. Like his sermons, they are filled with Old Testament references. Although he has paid an enormous price to step beyond the thoroughly Jewish world he grew up in, he still thinks like a Jewish man of his time. He must substantiate from the Old Testament everything he understands and feels. He particularly loves the story of Noah. It is the only story referred to in both Peter's letters—understandable for a man who grew up in a boat!

The letters display Peter's unique and often graphic vocabulary. Again and again he stresses the passionate need to "love one another deeply." His language becomes particularly harsh when he describes "proud and arrogant" men who are causing harm to the church. Age and years of hardship on the mission trail have not dimmed the passionate intensity of the man we first came to know in the Gospels.

OPEN

If you could write only two letters between now and the end of your life, to whom would you write? What would you write about?

STUDY

Read 1 Peter 3:8-9.

⁸Finally, all of you should be of one mind, full of sympathy toward each other, loving one another with tender hearts and humble minds. ⁹Don't repay evil for evil. Don't retaliate when people say unkind things about you. Instead, pay them back with a blessing. That is what God wants you to do, and he will bless you for it.

1. Consider Peter's word "finally" (v. 8). What does that word say to you about all that follows?

2. How does Jesus Christ perfectly demonstrate these qualities?

3. What do you think it would be like to belong to a church that lives by Peter's advice in this passage?

4. From your knowledge of Peter's life, how did he live up to his own words?

Peter's letters represent a poignant farewell. Jesus had earlier told him about the manner of his death, had strongly hinted that it would entail crucifixion (John 21:18). Now he has been given to understand that his own "exodus" is near (2 Peter 1:13-15). So, remarkably, we have in the letters, especially the second letter, Peter's last will and testament. *Read 2 Peter 1:5-8.*

⁵So make every effort to apply the benefits of these promises to your life. Then your faith will produce a life of moral excellence. A life of moral excellence leads to knowing God better. ⁶Knowing God leads to self-control. Self-control leads to patient endurance, and patient endurance leads to godliness. ⁷Godliness leads to love for other Christians, and finally you will grow to have genuine love for everyone. ⁸The more you grow like this, the more you will become productive and useful in your knowledge of our Lord Jesus Christ.

5. How do the spiritual qualities in this passage build on one another?

6. Why do you think faith must come *before* moral excellence (v. 5)?

7. What do you think it means to "become productive and useful" in your knowledge of the Lord (v. 8)?

8. From your knowledge of Peter's life, which of these qualities were the most difficult for him to realize?

9. Which of these qualities is most difficult for you to realize in your life?

10. Where, with the Holy Spirit's help, have you seen progress?

COMMIT

It is widely believed that Peter traveled to Rome in response to a request from Paul to help with a problem in the church at Rome. While Peter was there, he was caught up in the persecution of the church by Nero, around the time of the great fire in July of 64. Sources agree that Paul and Peter died at the same time. And so the fragile stone was finally broken, crucified upside down. It is said Peter requested this peculiar form of crucifixion because he considered himself unworthy to die in the same way Jesus had.

From simple fisherman to struggling disciple to first confessor, from despairing denier to fearless leader, from ambitious go-getter to humble servant. The progression (though infinitely more complicated) goes something like that. It is indeed miraculous that Jesus chose someone like Peter, a man we all identify with in one way or another, a person who teaches us more through his weaknesses than his strengths.

He humbly turns the title "Rock," which eventually became his true name, into an invitation, for in his eyes we are all supposed to be "living stones." But without a doubt, he was the first of these stones to be laid, the foundational disciple.

If we are to be "living stones," if the church is to go on being built the way Jesus desires it to be built, then Peter's story must in some sense become our story. Only then will our story become like Peter's, the story of Jesus.

Praise God for the example of Peter, and thank him that along with Peter, you are part of Christ's household, built on the solid foundation of Christ. A good closing activity would be to sing some hymns that include the word *rock*, such as "The Solid Rock" or "Rock of Ages."

Thank the Lord that even when you fail him, you have the example of how he forgave and restored Peter. Pray that you will always stand firm in Christ.

FOR FURTHER READING: chapter 18 & epilogue of *A Fragile Stone.*

Leader's Notes

This study guide can be used several ways. It can be the basis for a book discussion group in which each member is reading Michael Card's book *A Fragile Stone*. If this is the case, you as a group leader may not need to read out loud the book excerpts in each study. In addition to the discussion questions provided, you may want simply to ask group members questions like, "What parts of this chapter struck you the most? Did you underline or highlight anything that was particularly meaningful to you?"

On the other hand, the guide can also be used as an inductive Bible study on the life of Peter. Here you may be leading a small group where the members have probably not read the book. In that case, you may want to have someone read the book excerpt out loud during each session. Or you may give members a few moments to read the passage on their own. Because the book excerpts can be lengthy, you may not have time to read all the material aloud.

STUDY ONE.
A MEETING ON THE SEASHORE. LUKE 5:1-11.

PURPOSE: To be willing to let Christ disrupt our security and make us his followers.

QUESTION 2. Jesus begins by asking a favor. He asks to use one of their boats to give himself room, away from the crush of the crowd—and perhaps to keep from being pushed into the lake! Using a boat for a pulpit was an imaginative way to help the disciples begin to make the transition from being fishers of fish to fishers of men. (This is not the only time Jesus will preach from a boat. See Mk 4:1.)

QUESTION 3. Jesus was known as a carpenter and a teacher, not a fisherman. What he offers Simon is not some idle fishing advice but a confident command, as if he knows exactly where the fish are.

QUESTION 4. Peter, the only disciple who ever says "no" to Jesus, comes dangerously close this time as well. His response to Jesus is almost a no. The only reason he gives for obeying, "If you say so," will in time become the guiding principle for his life. The simple command of Jesus will be all it takes to move Peter. He has spent the last year getting to know his new Friend. Not long ago he witnessed the healing of his own mother-in-law. But now there is still a tone of reluctant obedience in Simon's voice.

QUESTION 5. It's as if the fish have appeared from out of nowhere, as if they have been dropped into the nets from out of the blue Galilean sky. It's the kind of catch of which legends are made, a net-ripping catch! In response to the miraculous catch, Peter asks for what he really does not want—he asks for Jesus to leave. He has become the frightened fish, thrashing in the net, wanting only to get away, or at least for Jesus to get away from him. Peter has come face to face with the frightening possibility of complete success. Failure, like their earlier empty nets, seems so much safer and predictable.

QUESTION 7. Jesus' word is crucial. "Fear not!" Our sinfulness will ultimately be dealt with. Now, because of his coming, our sin can never stand between us and Jesus. Peter's confession of his sinfulness means he is precisely the man for whom Jesus is looking. In fact, he is the first person to confess his sinfulness to Jesus.

STUDY TWO.
THE FEARLESS WATER WALKER. MATTHEW 14:22-33.

PURPOSE: To venture to do the impossible in response to the Lord's call.

QUESTION 3. Compare Jesus' reassuring words with his words to Peter in
Luke 5:10 (study 1).

Jesus walking on the sea is a divine revelation of who he is. He has just
fed the five thousand, revealing himself to be the "prophet like Moses"
(Deut 18). As the people received the bread some of them began to mur-
mur, "Could this be the prophet (like Moses)?" Although we will later
see that the disciples had missed the connection, at least some of the
people in the crowd had begun to understand. Now Jesus walks on the
water. Mark's detail that he was "passing by" hearkens back to Exodus
33:22, when God revealed himself to Moses by placing him in the cleft of
the rock and causing his glory to "pass by." Walking on the water was an
undeniable demonstration of what Job 9:8 speaks about: "He alone has
spread out the heavens and marches on the waves of the sea."

QUESTION 4. Peter's peculiarly worded question shows that he is beginning to understand that it is only the call of Jesus that will make the im-
possibility of walking on the water possible. With all that he doesn't
know, Simon somehow does understand that the call must originate
with Jesus. This explains the clumsy wording of his request. "If it's you,
tell me to come to you," he shouts above the howling wind. Bonhoeffer
says that discipleship is never an offer we make to Christ. It is only the
call of Jesus that makes everything possible.

QUESTION 5. Peter looked around at reality and began to do what he
should have naturally done under the influence of gravity when he first
climbed down out of the boat: he began to sink. In the very midst of the
miracle he doubts the new reality he has just stepped into, and it all starts
to unravel. He apparently had no doubt when he stepped out on the water. He asked for no proof beyond the sound of Jesus' command to come
to him. Without proof he walked on the water. When he saw the waves,
he began to need proof that the impossible he was doing could somehow
be possible. But what proof could there be that the impossible had be-

come possible besides actually doing the impossible? There is no proof great enough to prevent doubt. If you base your belief on proof, sooner or later you too will sink!

QUESTION 8. Jesus and the half-soaked Peter climb into the boat, and the wind, as if exhausted as well, dies down. And then something even more extraordinary occurs. Up till this time in Matthew's Gospel, Jesus has been worshiped by the Magi, by a leper and by a ruler of the synagogue. At the first storm the disciples wondered, "Who is this man?" Now they have begun to know. We have never heard or seen the disciples worshiping him until this moment. "Truly you are the Son of God!" they confess. The cumulative weight of all the revelation—the feeding of the five thousand, walking on the water and now the calm Jesus' presence provides after the windstorm—have convinced the disciples of his real identity.

STUDY THREE.
WHO THEY BOTH ARE. MATTHEW 16:13-23.

PURPOSE: To recognize Jesus as the Christ and to find our true identity in him.

BACKGROUND. Caesarea Philippi was the site of the ancient city of Paneas. The name of the city was derived from the god Pan. A limestone cave was there containing an altar where the pagan deity was worshiped by Syrian Greeks. Later Herod the Great would change the name of the town in honor of Augustus Caesar. There he would build a temple where Augustus would be worshiped as a god. The temple was near the grotto of Pan. The area was no doubt filled with pagan associations for both Jesus and his disciples. In light of the surroundings, this is the perfect place to hear the affirmation that it is neither Pan nor Augustus but Jesus who is the Son of the living God.

QUESTION 2. Luke tells us Jesus had been praying in a private place before the discussion with his disciples (9:18). Matthew simply says he asked, "Who do people say the Son of Man is?" Jesus has consistently referred to himself by means of this prophetic title. There is clearly no confusion among the disciples as to the fact that he is referring to himself.

It is important to realize that Jesus is not asking the question to gain information. John has made it clear that Jesus does not need to ask people questions (Jn 2:24-25). He is, in fact, offering the disciples an opportunity to confess who they believe him to be. His asking should be seen as the granting of an opportunity to take the next step in their faith and understanding of who he is.

QUESTION 3. Here, as in so many other places, Peter speaks for the Twelve. Had he not opened his mouth, the pain of the silence would have been unbearable for everyone, especially Jesus. There is a barely perceptible but highly significant shift in the tone of Peter's reply. He does not directly answer the question as Jesus asked it. That is, he does not preface his statement with the words "We say you are . . ." Instead, he openly and forcefully confesses the fact, "You are the Christ, the Son of the Living God." In spite of his strict Jewish monotheism, Peter is willing to ascribe divinity to Jesus. To say he is God's Son is to suggest that he is God. What an incredible leap of faith this took!

All that human wisdom could offer at this point was confusion and opposition to who Jesus was. If the truth were to be spoken, God would have to speak it, as indeed he had at the baptism of Jesus. Now he has graciously chosen to speak through the fragile stone that is Simon, the son of Jonah. The confession is not to be understood as an achievement by Peter. It is all God's doing, speaking through his servant.

QUESTION 4. Simon has not somehow won his title by his superior insight. In just a moment he will betray his lack of understanding and speak, in almost the same breath, on behalf of Satan. No, by grace, God has chosen to speak the truth about his Son through Peter. Jesus, in his graciousness, blesses Peter for what he is not ultimately responsible for. This will be the pattern of his and all the disciples' service for Jesus for the rest of their lives, as it remains ours today. Jesus begins to build the church on the first person who, by faith, confesses who he is. Millions will follow through the ages.

QUESTIONS 5 AND 6. For Peter as well as the other disciples, to be the Messiah clearly implies a throne and eternal glory for Jesus. What Peter does not understand is that before the glory there must come the Passion, the suffering and death of the Christ. Peter should not be looked down on for his naiveté. All the disciples—in fact, practically everyone in Judea—believed the same. They were the products of the popular teaching of the Pharisees who said that the Christ would not suffer. All of the prophetic passages in the Old Testament, which speak of the suffering of Jesus (called the "suffering servant of the Lord" passages, Ps 22; 69; Is 53) the Pharisees applied to themselves. In their minds they were the Lord's suffering servants. How could the Messiah ever possibly experience suffering? It defied all human logic. But Jesus always did and always will.

QUESTION 7. "This will never happen to you!" Peter blurts out as he tries to imagine the unimaginable. That is Satan's great hope, of course, that Jesus will not go to the cross, will not suffer for the sins of the world. And so for the moment Peter has become Satan's dark spokesman.

STUDY FOUR.
"FEAR NOT!" MARK 9:2-10.

PURPOSE: To be assured that a believer in Christ does not have to be afraid of God.

QUESTION 3. Jesus' transfiguration will become the most powerful revelation of his glory that any of the disciples will ever see. When they witness the cross, all they will see is a man being tortured to death. The glorious resurrection will not be witnessed by anyone except two angels. This moment of transfiguration will be the only revelation of the true nature of his glory until the parousia—his coming again in clouds of glory.

QUESTION 5. The traditional interpretation takes the word for "tent" (NLT "shrine") to refer to the booths that were set up to commemorate the Festival of Tabernacles (also known as Feast of Booths or *Sukkoth*). Seen in this light, Peter is inviting Moses and Elijah to stay a little longer and celebrate the feast together. Zechariah 14:16-19 speaks of booths as being a part of the celebration of the final kingdom. Perhaps Peter believes this really is the final moment, the coming of the kingdom of God. Were you and I to witness what he saw, perhaps we might believe the same thing.

A newer and, it seems to me, more likely interpretation is that the tents Peter proposes building are more in line with the tabernacle. The Greek word he uses is also used in the Septuagint to describe the tabernacle of Moses. Isn't Moses standing there, after all? Is he not, once again, meeting with God? And didn't Moses himself experience a sort of transfiguration at Sinai? (See Ex 34:29-35.) If all this is true, then what Peter has in mind is not extending their time together in some sort of religious holiday. He is trying, though incorrectly, to deal with his terror. He knows that no one could see the unveiled glory of God and live. In this interpretation the tents are meant to veil the radiance of the three holy figures in order to protect Peter and his companions.

QUESTION 6. God provides a cloud to envelop and protect the disciples. During their earthly ministries, both Moses and Elijah had encountered this cloud. Both of them had heard the voice of God (Deut 18:15; 1 Kings 17:2). Matthew tells us that the disciples fell face down, terrified, when they heard the Voice. Luke says they were terrified as they entered the cloud. The cloud is said to have "overshadowed" them. This is the same word that was used of the Spirit of God "overshadowing" Mary at the moment of the incarnation. The voice Jesus heard at his baptism, at the inauguration of his ministry, is heard once more as he nears its completion, as he makes ready for his "exodus" (Lk 9:31).

QUESTION 9. Whenever Jesus is revealed to them, those are always the first words on his lips. When the nets were miraculously filled, he looked down at the kneeling Peter and said, "Don't be afraid; from now on you'll catch men." When he calmed the demonic storm on the sea he asked, "Why were you afraid?" As he approached their boat, walking on the water, he called out, "I am, don't be afraid." And now as the terror is draining from their faces he speaks those same comforting words. When later he is raised from the dead, he will speak them to the women at the tomb: "Don't be afraid."

STUDY FIVE.
CONFUSION AT THE FINAL MEAL. JOHN 13:1-11.

PURPOSE: To see Jesus as the Servant Lord and to imitate him.

QUESTION 3. If you look closely at the story usually referred to as "the washing of the disciples' feet," you'll see that it is actually the story of the washing of Peter's feet. He and Jesus are the only two characters on the stage at this point. Jesus' demeanor betrays no bitterness toward the ones who will shortly betray him; there is in him no sense of approaching danger. He slowly makes his way around the triclinium, or three-sided table. He is dressed like a slave. He is acting like a slave. Peter's first statement in verse 6 is emphatic in the Greek: "You . . . my feet . . . wash!"

QUESTION 5. Perhaps Peter's tone is surly here, taking into account his difficult and disappointing day. Simon, we recall again, is the only one of the disciples who ever says "no" to Jesus. At this moment it is not a rejection of Jesus' friendship. It is a denial of who he really is: their Servant Lord. In essence, Peter is trying to say to Jesus, "You just don't get it, do you? This is not appropriate. Of all the inappropriate things that you've done, this is the most inappropriate." In order to enter into the emotional dimension of the story, we must first see how right in his own eyes Peter was to protest! Jesus is asking him to submit in humility to his servant lordship. Of all that he had been asked to do in the previous three years, this is the most difficult for Simon. Remember, Peter had only recently seen Jesus transfigured on Tabor.

QUESTION 6. Jesus' tone becomes more severe. "Unless I wash you, you have no part with me." Peter's denial is serious business. Jesus hinges his salvation, his discipleship on it. But for Peter in his confusion, this no doubt feels like more rejection. Jesus' point is that if Peter denies the humility of his Servant Savior, he cannot possibly take part in what Jesus is doing. His refusal to be served by Jesus renders him unusable as a future servant of Jesus. Until Peter submits to who Jesus really is, how can he become one of his disciples? For that matter, how can we?

Too often the complex tangle of Peter's emotional life is oversimplified. But here clearly his passion causes him to go overboard. "Then wash my hands and head as well, Lord, not just my feet!" Though he clearly did so a moment ago, he does not mean to say "no" to Jesus. If he could take back those vehement words, he would do so now.

STUDY SIX.
THE DESPAIRING DENIER. MARK 14:27-42, 66-72.

PURPOSE: To admit our denials of Christ and to resolve to acknowledge him openly.

QUESTION 1. The Eleven arrived together at the estate called Gethsemane. This was a resting place that Jesus frequented. It may have been owned by one of his wealthier followers, perhaps the same man who loaned them the upper room for their Passover. The setting, in the grove of olive trees, away from the crush of the city, provided the kind of peaceful surroundings Jesus favored. In A.D. 70, Titus would strip the flanks of the Mount of Olives during the siege of Jerusalem, using most of the wood for crosses. But the garden Peter rested in now was lined with terraces of olive trees.

QUESTION 2. Jesus' predictions of the disciples' failing have become more narrowly focused on Peter. It is unfair to assume that the tone of Peter's assertions in verses 33 and 35 are boastful. He is bewildered by the cumulative weight of Jesus' statements. What he affirms he believes in his heart to be true.

QUESTION 4. Jesus leaves eight of his disciples at the entrance to the garden with no instructions but "Sit here." He then takes the Three further into the garden and into his confidence. They have not been asked along simply because of Jesus' need for companionship during this dark time. They are asked to stay close in order to keep a watch. The soldiers will be coming shortly. (When they do arrive, it will be Jesus who first detects their coming, not the three incompetent lookouts.)

QUESTION 5. Though all three are soundly asleep, it is only Simon whom Jesus castigates. You can hear the tired disappointment in his voice: "Simon, couldn't you stay awake?" Earlier Peter had sworn he would follow Jesus to prison and even to death. Now he could not find it in himself to stay awake to watch with his agonizing Friend. Jesus, however, in the midst of his suffering, returns to make sure they are not falling into temptation. He had been praying for Peter (Lk 22:31-32). Now he instructs Peter to pray for himself. Without the prayers of Jesus we would not know his salvation. When Jesus says that the spirit is willing but the flesh is weak, it's possible that he was referring to both his own and the disciples' struggles.

QUESTION 8. One of the subtle indications that the Gospel of Mark came largely from the preaching of Peter is that, most often, when he is portrayed it is in humility or downright humiliation. Peter will not allow Mark to hide the failure of his denials, but there is still an incredible omission in Mark's version of the story as well as all the other Gospels except Luke. Upon Peter's third denial, only Luke tells us that Jesus turned and looked at Simon across the courtyard. As their eyes met, Peter remembered Jesus' prediction that Peter would deny him. It was, I believe, this look that broke Peter's heart.

The understanding gaze of Jesus could not have been one of disdain or condemnation. That was not Jesus' way. After all, Jesus would be condemned for Peter. I believe the only look that could have broken Simon as it did was one of love and forgiveness. Which is just what we would expect from the Savior.

STUDY SEVEN.
NEW HOPE ON THE SEASHORE. JOHN 21:1-19.

PURPOSE: To find renewed hope in the risen Christ.

QUESTION 1. In both cases Simon and some others had fished all night and caught nothing. In both cases Jesus surprised them by telling them to try again and giving them specific directions. In both cases they got a huge, unexplainable catch, and Peter responded radically as he recognized who Jesus was.

QUESTION 3. Jesus had been coming and going from their lives for a score of days. Evaporating through locked doors, miraculously appearing with the equivalent of a simple "Hi" on his lips. And yet, though they "knew" it was Jesus, at the same time they didn't ever fully know. Mary thought he was the gardener. His familiar voice made her certain it was Jesus. The disciples on the road to Emmaus didn't recognize him either, even though they talked with him for hours about the promises in the Old Testament. Their eyes weren't opened till he broke the bread, and then he vanished once more. It was never his face he pointed to when he wanted them to recognize him. It was always his wounds. This morning he shouts—perhaps mischievously?—to them, "Don't you even have a bite to eat?" And then it happens . . . again. Suddenly the boat lists hard to starboard and the ropes creak. Looking not at Jesus but at the fish-filled nets, John gasps, out of breath, "It's the Lord!" If it weren't for the first miraculous catch of fish, he never would have recognized Jesus at the second.

QUESTION 4. Unlike the time he saw Jesus walking on this same lake, Peter does not call out and boldly ask if he might walk on the water. Instead he throws his fisherman's coat on and dives into the chilly water. Does he wonder if he might walk again across the water? Is that why he jumps in with all his clothes on? Apparently John doesn't think we need to know. What is certain is that there was not a molecule of reluctance in Simon's heart. He *had* to get to Jesus. What's a hundred-yard swim in the cold morning water if it means being beside *him?*

QUESTION 6. When the final question came, Peter understood that Jesus was making a point. Three times the question had come. Three times Peter had denied him. Jesus is not only the perfect Savior; he is also the perfect Friend. He has commanded them to forgive; now he will perfectly demonstrate it. Painful as the questions are, they are an expression of Jesus' creative forgiveness.

The forgiveness of Jesus empowers Peter. Now he understands that his position of leadership is founded not on his strength but on his brokenness. Peter's love must be the greatest because he has been forgiven of the greatest sin. Even in this Peter ranks first among the disciples.

Once it is firmly established in his heart, he will be fit to lead them.

QUESTION 9. Jesus gives to Peter what all of us want and do not want at
the same time: a prophecy of his own death. Jesus knows that in time Peter will need the kind of confidence that only this sort of word can give.
His death, when it finally comes, will have been foreseen by Jesus decades earlier.

The key phrase of Jesus' prophecy is "stretch out your hands." In
those words Peter would have doubtless heard a reference to crucifixion.
Epictetus wrote, "Stretch yourselves out like men who have been crucified" (*Disc* 3.26.22). Seneca spoke of "others stretching out their arms on
a cross beam" (*Consol ad Marciam* 20:3). The two terms most often used to
refer to crucifixion were "to be lifted up" and "to be stretched out." Peter
would be crucified like Jesus, only when the time came, he would beg to
be "stretched out" upside down. He did not feel worthy to die like Jesus.

STUDY EIGHT.
THE RELUCTANT RECONCILER. ACTS 10:1-36.

PURPOSE: To reach out in reconciliation to those who are not like us.

QUESTIONS 1 AND 2. The incident takes place deep in enemy territory.
Caesarea was the Roman capital of Judea. The fact that the object of the
story is a high-ranking Roman officer makes matters even worse. He
represents all that is loathsome to the Jews. But then again we are told
that he was "devout." The technical term "God-fearer" (indicating that
he was a Gentile who worshiped the God of Israel but would not submit
to circumcision in order to become a full proselyte) is used to describe
his intimate relationship to Judaism. He also practices two of the central
tenets of Jewish piety: he gives to the poor and observes the regular
hours of prayer.

All this being true, the fact remains that he is still Roman and a Gentile. Despite his affinity for Judaism, no observant Jew would have shared a meal with him, nor even entered into his house. It is important to note that God sent a vision to both Cornelius and Peter to help prepare them for their life-changing experiences.

QUESTION 4. In Acts 9:43 we are told that Peter was staying in Joppa beside the sea, in the house of a man named Simon. This would not be so unusual until we read that he was a tanner, that is, his job was skinning animals and preparing the hides. This meant that he was constantly in contact with unclean carcasses and their blood, and so was considered perpetually unclean. Peter's choice of accommodations reveals that some of his old concerns about his ritual purity were beginning to shift.

QUESTION 5. Peter falls into a trance, literally an "ecstasy." He sees heaven open and a large sheet or perhaps a sail being lowered down to him. To his amazement and disgust, the sail is filled with unclean animals, with all the things he has spent a lifetime avoiding. If indeed it was a sail that he saw, we see the imagination of God at work, wrapping up what was unfamiliar in something familiar that Peter had known and used every day.

QUESTION 7. Peter goes down to meet them and hears for the first time a story he will retell for the rest of his life. Since it is evening, he makes the remarkable gesture of inviting them into the house to stay the night. The only thing worse than a tanner's house is a tanner's house full of Gentiles!

QUESTION 10. What an earthquake in Peter's soul! It was a direct assault on one of his most basic beliefs. But Jesus had come to shatter and redefine everything. Certainly it is a shattered Simon who makes his way, for the first time in his life, into this Gentile dwelling. He will find there men and women, like himself, who want nothing less than to eat the true bread of heaven. People who, though they live in darkness, have nonetheless seen a great Light!

STUDY NINE.
THE PASSIONATE WRITER. 1 PETER 3:8-9; 2 PETER 1:5-8.

PURPOSE: To see how Peter's letters encapsulate his ministry and his friendship with Christ.

QUESTION I. Peter's two letters were written to a mixed group of Gentile and Jewish Christians, an appropriate flock for a shepherd who had sacrificed so much to bring the two together. They lived in and around Asia Minor in the areas of Pontus, Galatia, Cappadocia, Asia and Bithynia. This is the area Paul was forbidden to enter in Acts 16:7 (see also Rom 15:20). The listing of these areas is the only hint we have of the focus of Peter's missionary activity in the later years of his life.

QUESTION 5. This statement has been rightly called the "Ladder of Faith," for each concept builds on the former (Paul delighted in the same type of "chain sayings": Rom 5:3-5; Gal 4:4-7; 1 Tim 6:11-12). The bookends of this remarkable statement (a statement that requires a lifetime to meditate on and understand): *faith* and *love*. These might be said to be the bookends of Peter's own spiritual journey. What began with a remarkable statement of faith at Caesarea Philippi ended in a missionary life defined and dominated by love.

For more information about
the ministry and music of Michael Card, contact:

The Card Group LLC
(615) 790-7675
E-mail: info@michaelcard.com
Or go to: www.michaelcard.com

About the Authors

MICHAEL CARD is an award-winning musician, performing artist and the writer of many popular songs, including the classics "El Shaddai" and "Immanuel." He has produced over twenty albums, including *Scribbling in the Sand: The Best of Michael Card Live* and his latest release, *A Fragile Stone*. He is also the author of numerous books, including *Scribbling in the Sand* and *The Parable of Joy*.

Card has been a mentor to many younger artists and musicians, teaching courses on the creative process and calling the Christian recording industry to deeper discipleship. He lives in Tennessee with his wife and four children.

Card holds an undergraduate degree in biblical studies from Western Kentucky University (1979). He also had an assistantship and taught physics and astronomy in a master's program at WKU. Michael went on to receive a master's degree in biblical studies from Western Kentucky University in 1980. He is currently working on his doctorate in classical literature.

In cooperation with The Bible League, Michael Card has launched the Michael Card Share the Word Project to provide Bibles to persecuted Christians and searching people. For over ten years Card has partnered with The Bible League's efforts to supply Bibles to people around the world. For more information, contact The Michael Card Share the Word Project, c/o Bible League, P.O. Box 28000, Chicago, IL 60628, or e-mail info@bibleleague.org or visit <www.mcsharetheword.org>.

DALE AND SANDY LARSEN are the authors of numerous books and Bible study guides, including *7 Myths About Christianity*, *A Woman of Grace* and the *Scribbling in the Sand Study Guide*. They are the founders of Merritt Park Press (www.merrittpark.com) and live in southern Illinois.

ALSO AVAILABLE
FROM INTERVARSITY PRESS

A FRAGILE STONE: *The Emotional Life of Simon Peter*
Exploring the dynamic, contradictory life of the apostle Peter, Michael
Card shows how the impetuous fisherman of Galilee was transformed into
a pivotal leader of the early church. He offers hope that we likewise can be
radically changed as Jesus calls us to follow him. *200 pages, cloth, 0-8308-2372-7,
$17.00. A Fragile Stone Audio Book,* read by the author. *Two 80-minute CDs, 0-8308-
2373-5, $20.00.*

SCRIBBLING IN THE SAND: *Christ and Creativity*
Michael Card explores the biblical foundation of true Christian creativity
and invites you to follow God's creative call through worship and commu-
nity. *168 pages, cloth, 0-8308-2317-4, $16.00.* Also available: *Scribbling in the Sand Study
Guide,* 8 studies for individuals or groups. *78 pages, paper, 0-8308-2059-0, $6.00;
Scribbling in the Sand Audio Book,* read by the author, with exclusive interviews
and extra material not available in the book. *Two 80-minute CDs, 0-8308-2303-4,
$20.00.*

For more information about *A Fragile Stone* and its related products, visit
<www.afragilestone.com>.